Taking Back Our Lives

Taking Back Our Lives

Reflections for Survivors
of Child Abuse

Patti Sherlock

ACTA

ASSISTING CHRISTIANS TO ACT

PUBLICATIONS

Taking Back Our Lives
Reflections for Survivors of Child Abuse
by Patti Sherlock

Edited by Kass Dotterweich
Cover design and photo by Tom A. Wright
Typesetting by Desktop Edit Shop, Inc.

Scripture quotations are from the New Revised Standard Version of the Bible, copyright © 1989 by the Division of Christian Education of the National Council of the Churches of Christ in the U.S.A. Used with permission. All rights reserved.

Published by: ACTA Publications
Assisting Christians To Act
4848 N. Clark Street
Chicago, IL 60640-4711
773-271-1030

Library of Congress Card Number: 20022116539
ISBN: 0-87946-239-6
Printed in the United States of America
Year: 07 06 05 04 03 / Printing: 7 6 5 4 3 2 1

Contents

Dedication

When I was a young child, three little girls from my neighborhood used to confide separately to me astonishing tales from their families. The stories involved a father in one case, a stepfather and a brother in another, and uncles in the third. These males, the girls said, possessed an outlandish body part and forced the girls to participate in activities that, when they told of them, filled their eyes with fear and hate. The girls whispered these secrets, and I respected their confidence. I never told anyone. Although I did not think the girls were lying, I earnestly hoped they had gotten their facts wrong.

Across the street from us lived a family of three: a couple and their teenage daughter. Periodically, the man got drunk and chased the woman and the young girl into the front yard, where he bellowed, threatened and hit them while they begged him to stop. Several times on such occasions, the police showed up. The woman often wore shiners, and the girl, popular in high school, struggled to camouflage her bruises.

When I was in junior high, I began babysitting for a family with three children. The mother and father were pleasant, but they worked long and peculiar hours and the kids lived in grimy neglect. Mice and insects overran the house, swarming over kitchen chairs and counters. The kids wore soiled clothing and went without routine hygiene.

Viewed against these situations, my family didn't seem particularly strange, though I endured thrashings with tree limbs, blows to the head, threats with knives, and verbal humiliations. Regularly, I was shuffled off to live with relatives; twice my older sister and I were sent to an orphanage. After the lights were out at the orphanage, children in my ward whimpered and cried, and I would bury my nose in the sheets in an attempt to avoid the smell of urine. Fear filled the darkness for all of us.

> Fear filled the darkness for all of us.

I usually walked to school and on my way passed through neat subdivision neighborhoods. As I passed one lovely yard after another, I would find myself imagining the tidy and tranquil lives of children who lived in those homes. By contrast, my own rural neighborhood was financially strapped. Although we had adequate food and a car to drive, no money was available for extras. When I was a little older and started going to birthday parties in those subdivision neighborhoods, I had my thinking confirmed. The subdivision daughters were allowed to wear their good shoes on weekdays, their mothers smiled incessantly and called them "Darling," and there were no signs of violence or dreaded uncles anywhere.

Even in my very own neighborhood, some families struck me as enviable. One girl in particular spoke so fondly of her parents it made me ache. She adored her brothers and she chattered on and on about the Catholic church she attended. She wore white doilies on her head on Sunday and waved and smiled at me from her car as the family drove off to Mass.

In my mind, I lived worlds distant from the Catholic girl and the subdivision girls. My world was a dark secret, so secret that parts of it became hidden even from me.

As a young reporter many years later, I covered a child abuse case that involved people from the "good" side of town. The Health Department suspected the father, who was a doctor, and the mother, who was a former model, of killing their baby. The social worker hoped the newspaper could unearth evidence to substantiate this suspicion, because he worried that the couple's three other children might be in danger as well. As it turned out, despite neighbors observing violence in that family for years, the police were not able to produce concrete evidence. I don't know what happened to the other children.

Looking back now, I realize what a long and entrenched habit of denial I had developed.

During that period, statistics on child abuse gained national attention. My neighborhood, which I had believed aberrant in the extreme, turned out to be statistically typical.

When I reached mid-life and finally sought counseling for the abuse I had suffered as a child, I was shocked to learn how much those early experiences had followed me into adulthood. Until that time, I had seen my adult life as productive and happy. Looking back now, I realize what a long and entrenched habit of denial I had developed.

Sometimes I think of the little girls I grew up with, of their whispered tales and darting eyes. I recall the three children who lived in abject filth. I wonder about the battered teenager and what became of her. I remember the sniffling children of the orphanage in their urine-soaked beds. I consider what tales of violence, humiliation and sexual trespass the subdivision children may have been concealing.

Wherever these people are today, I hope they have found help and support. To them, brave survivors all, I dedicate these reflections.

≋≋

Introduction

We number in the millions. We live in every country in the world. We differ from one another in many ways and represent a variety of cultural backgrounds. Some of us grew up rich, some poor; some of us came from religious homes, and some of us grew up without religious formation of any kind. Some of us earned advanced degrees; some never went to school. Although the circumstances of our upbringing vary, a common element connects us: we grew up scared.

Today they call us *survivors*, those of us who grew up with physical, sexual or emotional abuse. *Survivors* replaced the inaccurate term *victims*. "Victim" implied helplessness, a state we as children couldn't avoid. "Survivor" tells the present story—how we managed to endure, how we bore the pain, how we grew up despite the abuse visited upon us. As survivors we know our experiences gave us something valuable with regard to strength and empathy—and maybe dozens of other qualities. Yet fear often persists as the biggest legacy from our childhood, showing up in both routine and extraordinary situations. We find it hard to trust; we blame ourselves for difficulties beyond our control; we feel undeserving of respectful treatment; we shrink from success; we run from love. We are scared.

Again and again, our own fear ambushes us. We react strangely to a scene in a movie; we jump out of our skin when someone startles us; we find ourselves trembling when walking into a dark basement. Even today, as adults, we may find ourselves sweating when we hear the voice of our abuser on the telephone. When a newscaster reports that a child has been harmed by his or her caretakers, our hearts race, our stomachs lurch and our eyes spring tears. In our adult minds, we may understand that our caretakers acted wrongly, that they ought to have cherished and respected us when we were children. But vulnerable, frightened parts of our younger selves still harbor the sense that we got exactly what we deserved.

Those of us who are survivors of child abuse hide our fear in many ways.

Those of us who are survivors of child abuse hide our fear in many ways. We work hard to please—or we work at nothing. We behave like pleasers—or we get loud and intimidating. We wheedle or cower, threaten or grovel. We find an addiction to numb us. Sometimes our fear tells us to turn a cold shoulder to those we desire to hold closer. We may so completely deny the pain of childhood that we dissociate from it entirely and become partly or completely amnesiac.

Invariably, our fear will be reflected in how we practice our religious faith. We may be the wincing sort who trembles before a threatening deity, or we may have no interest whatsoever in things of the Spirit. As children, many of us based our idea of the Supreme Being on what we knew of the powerful people around us. If parents and caretakers were kind, dependable and accepting, we likely transferred those qualities to God. But when parents were a threat to our safety and well-being, we came to dread encounters with the Divine.

Yet we survivors who based part or all of our self-worth on how parents and caretakers treated us yearn for a confident and loving relationship with God. We sense that if we could grasp our importance in God's eyes, the heart wounds we carry would begin to close. But we don't know where to start. After all, isn't it possible that God, like the abusing parent, will reject us?

We can heal, and we can also regain or strengthen our spirituality if it was stifled by abuse.

Considering the great harm that results from childhood abuse, we may worry that we will not be able to escape its fallout through our adult years. But we can; help is available. The world has opened its eyes to the frequency and seriousness of child abuse. Legislators, doctors, teachers, social workers and the general public have become keenly alert to this often silent and hidden violence. Counselors have gained wide experience in helping survivors, and support groups abound. We can heal, and we can also regain or strengthen our spirituality if it was stifled by abuse.

This book of reflections intends to be a companion to those setting off on a healing journey to confront childhood trauma and recover from it—a journey that is by no means a straight-forward course. The road to healing is full of twists and turns, and the path often winds back onto itself, as we feel we've surely "been here before." The challenge always is to trust that no, we have not been here before. Although circumstances and feelings are familiar, we have taken some small step toward healthier living. Today, in any given situation, we are better prepared to respond with greater confidence. For that reason, the arrangement of these reflections is free of any definition regarding "steps" or "themes" or "categories." Rather, readers are invited to rely on the table of contents to lead them to the reflection they need at any given moment.

May those of us who have survived the darkness of childhood abuse come to appreciate that we were innocent in the abuse we suffered. May we grow to honor the great strength we've shown in surviving. Through healing, may we find a dynamic, healthy and faith-filled spirituality to provide a steady platform for the new life we are becoming free to choose.

≈≈

Taking Back My Life

The man stood in the middle of the group, shook his fist at the ceiling and declared, "I'm taking back my life. Do you hear me on this? I'm taking back my life!" I wrote down the words and posted them on my bathroom mirror when I got home.

The abusers of our childhood did, indeed, take away our trust and innocence. They stole our peace and confidence. They may be stealing our lives from us even yet.

Our abusers have destroyed enough in us.

When we pull back from opportunity because we worry we are not capable, when we run from a relationship because we fear relationships are ultimately painful, when we repudiate who we are because we think we can never be enough, we continue to let our abusers rob us of the fullness of life.

Our abusers have destroyed enough in us. We may choose to understand their reasons for doing what they did to us; we may choose to hate their reasons for what they did to us; we may choose to understand *and* hate what they did to us. But we do not have to let our abusers take away more of our precious days.

Today we can repudiate the old messages, declare how worthy and deserving we are, and commit to living life with energy and dynamism.

Stand and say it. Say it with conviction. Shake your fist. Yell. Cry if you need to. You have God's attention.

I am taking back my life. Do you hear me on this? I am taking back my life!

Here, in my own soul,
the greatest of all miracles has taken place—
God has returned to God!

—Meister Eckhart

∽∾

Getting It "Right"

We survivors of child abuse sometimes do not even have enough confidence that we can do our healing right.

If we devote a significant portion of our time to healing, we feel we are somehow cheating our families. If, on the other hand, we devote little time to healing, we scold ourselves for being lazy. If we see a therapist, we criticize ourselves over the money we're spending. If we do not see a therapist, we accuse ourselves of lacking commitment. If we try to heal on our own with the help of books and journals, we suspect we're inadequate to the task. If we participate in a support group, we notice that others seem to be making greater progress than we are.

We figured out that we couldn't change the abuser, but we could change ourselves.

And, of course, always there's fear. As children, we had a choice. Either the abuser was wrong, or we were wrong. As children, we accepted that we were wrong, because that was the more attractive choice. If the caretaker was wrong, then everything in the world was wrong and chaos reigned. But if we were wrong, at least there was the possibility that we could fix it. We could be compliant, give up noisiness and naughtiness, be less attractive, be inconspicuous. We could attempt to control our environment with rituals and formulas. In our juvenile wisdom, we figured out that we could not change the abuser, but we could change ourselves.

Today, as adults, we realize how much our sense of fear of not getting it "right" impedes our efforts at healing. We want to believe that God supports us along our journey, but a part of us worries that God is saying, "Ah, come on, is that the best you can do?"

Know that Spirit has all the time in the world.

Today let us affirm that our healing is progressing exactly as it needs to.

Be transformed by the renewing of your minds.
—Romans 12:2

Not Our Fault

It is so obvious that it goes without saying, but we need to say it again and again and again: "It wasn't my fault." The abuse we suffered as children was not our fault.

Intellectually, we know our childish blunders didn't warrant severe punishments. We know children don't lure sexual abusers. We know adults ought to resist speaking words that crush children's hearts and spirits. And yet...when something goes wrong at work, in our homes, or even on the other side of the world, we get an uneasy feeling that, once again, we've messed up. In our sessions with counselors and support groups, we hesitate to share details of abuse because we suspect our listeners will see that we brought it on ourselves. Throwing common sense to the wind, we sometimes defend our abusers and insist we only got what we deserved. We told lies, stole from the refrigerator, betrayed family secrets, spilled on carpets, and put nicks in the furniture.

We need to remind ourselves that we didn't provoke the treatment we got.

"I was a mouthy kid," the woman confesses, eyes filling. Her mother chopped off her hair and locked her in a closet.

We need to remind ourselves, a hundred times a day if necessary, that we didn't provoke the treatment we got. Our abusers found justification for unjustifiable actions. Consequently, we dragged into adulthood the belief that we are unworthy, undeserving and unlovable.

To reverse the pernicious aftermath of abuse, we must start to comprehend, at a deep level, how absolutely worthy and deserving we are. This is a compelling motive for working on our healing. When we understand how secure our place is in God's heart, we can claim our self-worth and inestimable value—to ourselves and others.

Today we can look in the mirror and state with conviction, "It was not my fault."

There is a part of every living being that wants to become itself;
the tadpole into a frog,
the chrysalis into the butterfly,
a damaged human being into a whole one.
That is spirituality.

—Ellen Bass

Taking Unfamiliar Roads

My friend worries that she will get lost in new and unfamiliar places. Recently, while visiting a nearby town, she decided to challenge her fear. She took a deep breath, admitted her anxiety and started down an unfamiliar street.

Within two blocks, my friend came to a street lined with people. An international folk-dancing festival had started that day, and scores of people had turned out to welcome the dancers. In colorful costumes, performers from around the world danced as they moved through the neighborhood to the delight of hundreds of spectators. My friend, who intended only a slight departure from the routine—just enough to push against her anxiety—found herself enjoying an exhilarating morning of entertainment, laughter, talent and cultural pride.

We make a choice to subdue fear, and we deliberately take a new and unfamiliar road.

The journey to health for survivors of child abuse resembles my friend's experience. We make a choice to subdue fear, and we deliberately take a new and unfamiliar road. Just a few blocks away, we can find a colorful parade that delights our spirits and rewards our courage to choose something different.

Not all ventures down new roads turn out so pleasurably, of course—but that, too, is part of our healing journey. Today let us anticipate bright surprises as we travel new and unfamiliar roads.

The Lord will keep your going out and your coming in.
—Psalm 121:8

Facing Yesterday's Reality Today

The man insisted that digging in the past is self-indulgent and unproductive. He was visiting a support group for survivors of abuse, but he announced right away that it wasn't for him. Rather, he offered the group an alternative: get on with life; enjoy the present; make peace with the past.

When a woman asked the man if that approach really worked for him, he insisted that it did. Well, he admitted, there was the matter of his shattered marriage, his workaholism, his collapsing business, the hostility toward his business partners and the estrangement from his mother. But of course none of that had anything to do with the abuse in his background.

It's understandable that we don't want to drag painful memories to the surface. Rather, we want to believe that time has healed us. We want to believe that we have conquered the pain of those early years, even if we've never revisited them. We can even deny that fallout from our abusive backgrounds exists at all. Yet a look at the disorder in our lives may tell us otherwise.

A friend of mine described her conversation with a terminally ill cancer patient. My friend tried so hard to avoid mentioning the word *cancer* that it pressed in on everything she said and thought. She used all her energy to stay away from the topic.

> *Then, one day, we make a decision to look at the truths of our past, because that honest look serves our best interest.*

In the same way, it costs us a great deal of effort to stay away from the sadness of our abuse. Then, one day, we make a decision to look at the truths of our past, because that honest look serves our best interest. We decide to remove the splinters from old wounds and allow them to close and heal. It is a brave and significant undertaking.

> *May those who sow in tears reap with shouts of joy.*
> *Those who go out weeping, bearing the seed for sowing,*
> *shall come home with shouts of joy, carrying their sheaves.*
> —Psalm 126:5-6

Feeling Cherished

As children, we want to believe that God cherishes us. We desperately long to feel that we have inestimable worth in the Creator's eyes. We want to think that God experiences our pain with us or, conversely, is delighted when we experience joy.

But those of us who are survivors of childhood abuse may not have much experience in feeling that we are cherished. Rather, our experience was more like that of shipwrecked sailors clinging to floating debris, grasping for anything to keep from drowning in a sea of fear and hopelessness. Our caretakers may even have told us we were the most important person in the world to them, but their violence and threats pierced our hearts and shattered the credibility of those declarations.

In so many ways, we were told that our birth was a mistake.

Mother said she gave up a good career to raise us and that we were a burden. Father complained that he endured an arduous job to support us, and he lashed out at us on weekends. In so many ways, we were told that our birth was a mistake.

Now we want to see ourselves as precious, but how do we do that?

We may have to grope our way at first. We may need to repeat affirmations we don't believe. We may have to act in ways that don't feel natural. We may have to imagine what we can't yet accept as true. Alcoholics Anonymous uses the slogan "Fake it till you make it." We can borrow that idea.

"If I could truly believe that I am cherished by God, then I could..." What? Take a risk? Get out of a destructive relationship? Pursue a satisfying career? Let myself have a nap because I'm tired?

"If I could know for certain that God loves me, I would..." What? Stop apologizing for myself? Stop driving myself like a pack mule? Give myself some credit for my accomplishments?

One way we can start believing we are loved and cherished is to cherish ourselves. We can acknowledge our strengths, forgive our mistakes and treat our emotions, bodies and souls with respect.

As though we were deeply cherished as children.

As though we are deeply cherished now.

For it was you who formed my inward parts;
you knit me together in my mother's womb.
I praise you, for I am fearfully and wonderfully made.
Wonderful are your works; that I know very well.
—Psalm 139:13-14

Learning to Run, Despite

I bought hobbles, a restraining device that fits a horse's front legs, so I could let my horse graze in a rich, unfenced field. I hoped the contraption wouldn't frighten her, so after I fitted it on her front ankles I hung around to comfort and reassure her if she needed it. But she calmly put her head down and began to eat. Then a few minutes later she inched ahead, untroubled by her constraints. I returned to my work, pleased that my horse could graze in the lush field.

> *My horse had figured out how to move despite the hobbles holding her front legs together.*

Less than an hour later, I saw a red horse gallop past my window. My mouth dropped. Surely it couldn't be *my* mare going at that speed. But it was. My horse had figured out how to move, even run, despite the hobbles holding her front legs together. I had to smile at the animal's accomplishment. Her natural high spirits weren't dampened by manacles.

I have sometimes been restricted in how fast or how well I could move. With old wounds and fears acting as impediments, inching ahead even slightly felt clumsy. But when I began to figure out my encumbrances, I started to move with greater freedom. I didn't have to make today's fears and wounds from the past disappear; I only needed to learn how to move despite them.

The abuse in our background may have hobbled us. That doesn't mean we can't run.

But those who wait for the Lord shall renew their strength,
they shall mount up with wings like eagles,
they shall run and not be weary,
they shall walk and not faint.

—Isaiah 40:31

Exposing Wounds

A man gets punched in the stomach and doubles over with pain. Later, when the doctor examines him for injuries, he must expose his stomach to prodding and poking, though he would prefer to remain huddled, arms covering his throbbing belly. He consents to a vulnerable position only because he believes the doctor is going to be helpful in alleviating some of the pain.

Dealing with old wounds from childhood abuse can be like this. We may have taken hard punches, emotionally and physically, and doubled over from the pain. Now, because something urges us toward healing, we're asked to expose our wounds. That can feel dangerous.

With help, the pain will be eased.

Of course we're reluctant to uncover tender places. Of course we don't want to tolerate poking and prodding. But our injuries may need attention—from us, a professional counselor or a support group. With help, the pain will be eased.

Do we want to remain huddled, or would we like to expose our wounds and eventually stand tall?

We know the answer already; that's why we've started on this path. We can surrender our protective posture, confident that a Higher Power wants to act as a helpful physician and touch our tender wounds with love.

From suffering I have learned this:
that whoever is sore wounded by love will never be made whole
unless she embrace the very same love which wounded her.
—Mechtilde of Magdeburg

Whose Voice Am I Listening To?

We survivors of child abuse watch ourselves edit our words or alter our actions to suit others. We say things we don't mean; we don't say things we wish we had; we agree to do things we don't want to do. At those times, we can move in the direction of healing by asking ourselves, "Whose voice am I listening to?"

The voice we hear may belong to a younger self who wants to be safe, accepted or loved. Sometimes the voice may belong to someone from our past: the third-grade teacher who called us stupid; the uncle who slapped us; the grandfather who whispered seductions in our ear.

We can stop these ancient voices and replace them with healthy, caring and accurate ones.

We can stop these ancient voices and replace them with healthy, caring and accurate ones: *I am bright. I am powerful. I deserve respectful treatment. I don't have to agree to anything*

I don't feel good about.

When we find ourselves behaving in ways that do not align with our highest aspirations, we can question whose voice we're listening to. If someone from our past is uttering untruthful messages, we can turn off that voice and turn on new messages based on the truth: we are worthy, lovable and deserving of a wonderful life. We can hold that view with confidence.

Become aware of what is in you.
Announce it, pronounce it, produce it and give birth to it.
—Meister Eckhart

A Close Companionship with God

The little boy huddled in his bed and prayed, "I'm sorry, God, for stealing bread from the kitchen. Please don't start World War III tonight."

This little boy lived in a violent home where parents administered severe punishment for mild misbehavior. In the course of a day, the child apologized often to those around him, and his prayers generally started with the words, "I am so, so sorry, God." Although he longed to feel connected to a friendly God, he remained fearful and distant because he expected God to impose severe punishments. The boy's prayers changed somewhat as he grew up, but he retained his attitude of fear. He couldn't help but expect that an angry deity would inflict terrible penalties for even the smallest of mistakes.

He became fearful of making mistakes in friendships, parenting and love.

As the boy grew into a man, he viewed his relationships with others the same way he had experienced his relationship with God. He became fearful of making mistakes in friendships, parenting and love. He dropped out of many relationships before he could be rejected.

One day a coworker challenged him to stop apologizing for things that weren't his fault or—if the situation were his fault—to apologize only once and then forget it. He tried, but it was too difficult, so he sought help in therapy.

In counseling, the young man began to heal from his abusive background; he stopped being so hard on himself. These days he enjoys a close companionship with God. Yes, there are times when he slips into old fears and becomes concerned that God may be an exacting tyrant, but most of the time he feels an intimate relationship with a warm, accepting deity.

Today we can ask God to help us accept ourselves and our humanity. We can be confident that God is not a calculating deity who doles out punishment for our misdeeds. Rather, God created us and loves us completely.

If I take the wings of the morning
and settle at the farthest limits of the sea,
even there your hand shall lead me,
and your right hand shall hold me fast.
—Psalm 139:9-10

Becoming Real

We survivors of child abuse learned to act the way others required or expected us to act. We smiled when we wanted to cry; we remained quiet when we wanted to yell; we held our mouths tightly shut when we wanted to laugh. We've now been artificial for so long that we don't even recognize our falseness. When someone suggests we're being Pollyannaish or stoic, overly controlled or fake, we deny it.

"I'm not upset, really."

"I've learned to not let things bother me."

"I seldom get angry anymore; it doesn't pay."

"I accept that it's for the best."

"I only want his/her happiness."

We sleepwalk through situations that would call forth tremendous response in a person who feels freer to express emotions. Conversely, because we suppress our feelings so strongly, we may explode like a volcano over something minor.

We don't want to express emotions in ways that harm or frighten others, of course. And we don't want to unleash strong emotions in inappropriate places or at inappropriate times.

But we rob ourselves of vitality and humanity when we quell powerful feelings and rein in emotions we consider unacceptable. We take our first steps in retrieving authentic feelings when we quit judging which emotions we'll allow ourselves to feel. We can start letting ourselves practice becoming real by expressing honest anger, giving in to tears, laughing out loud or admitting to fear.

Our magnificent hearts overflow with mighty emotions.

Our magnificent hearts overflow with mighty emotions. We are safe now—if not, we must find a way to become safe—and we can express real feelings.

I am a little pencil in the hand of a writing God
who is sending a love letter to the world.
—Mother Teresa of Calcutta

❧❧

Acknowledging the Scars

When we survivors of child abuse are working on healing, it feels like the past dominates our lives. We are hyperaware of how abuse continues to exert an influence on our present actions, emotions and choices. So when someone complains about "people who refuse to let go of the past" or "people who insist on nursing their victimhood," we reproach ourselves.

We learned how to make the best of things, how to pick ourselves up and carry on.

It would be good for us to remember that for years we behaved in an opposite way: we "let go of the past" completely. We refused to look at our past, insisting that our background hadn't hurt us much. Some of us expressed pride in the fact that we had come through so well. Many of us moved through life unaware that choices we were making as adults helped to perpetuate unhealthy attitudes from our childhood.

Did our denial serve us well? In ways, yes. We found a way

to not hurt so much. We learned how to make the best of things, how to pick ourselves up and carry on.

But how much energy did we expend pretending that we weren't hurt? How truthfully could we live while still in denial?

Until I acknowledged the scars from my past, I lived my days defensively—dodging conflict, apologizing and often feeling resentful because I didn't know how to stick up for myself. I expected to be slapped down if I acted too confident, punished if I made a mistake. I worked harder than others. I chose not to notice that I got frequent colds, didn't sleep well, and felt uneasy in many social situations. All the while, I insisted I was very, very happy.

When I at last began to face the truth in counseling, I did not acknowledge myself for bravery. Rather, I scolded myself for wasting time in self-centered examination. Yet, during times of meditation, when I tried to discern what God wanted for me, I got the answer to keep going in my therapy.

In times of doubt, we can ask for and expect to receive guidance about how to proceed. Often we will be nudged forward, toward healing.

Grace pours all beauty into the soul.
—Meister Eckhart

Holy Words, Unholy Purposes

onor thy father and thy mother." "Forgive seventy times seven." "Turn the other cheek." These words may express attractive concepts when applied in healthy situations, but child abusers use them to manipulate and control. "Spare the rod and spoil the child" expresses an unconscionable attitude, but one that has been widely embraced. It is tragic that even sexual abusers have found biblical passages to try to justify their behavior.

We are free to throw away the kind of religion that abusers used for purposes of manipulation.

In some cases, religious training counseled us to stifle anger and forgive, respect and honor those who violated us. The family, we were told, had sacred status, and God had granted unchallengeable power to parents. Some religious professionals even abused children themselves. Is it any wonder, then, that when we draw close to God we feel uneasy? Will God behave like the figures of authority we've known in the past? Is God angry that we lack warm sentiments toward our abusers?

We don't need to give up our spirituality, our faith. Rather, we can take a stand for ourselves and seek a spirituality that respects us as beloved persons with souls of inestimable value. We are free—right now—to throw away the kind of religion that abusers used for purposes of manipulation.

Love transforms.
Love makes empty hearts overflow.
This happens even more when we have to struggle through
without assurance, all unready
for the play of love.
—Mechtilde of Magdeburg

Wearing New Coats

My friend heard of a child in her son's class who didn't have a warm winter coat. The one the child wore to school was so threadbare and thin that he couldn't enjoy recess with his friends when Idaho weather turned cold.

My good-hearted friend found out from the teacher what style and color the boy preferred, then bought a beautiful blue coat and sent it to him anonymously for Christmas. The child loved his present.

Let us be patient with ourselves.

After school resumed in January, however, my friend learned that the boy was wearing his old coat. Concerned that one of the child's older siblings might have taken the coat away from him or that the boy might have lost the coat, the woman asked her son about the situation. "He likes his new coat, Mom," her son replied. "He's just used to the old one."

As survivors of child abuse, we sometimes don't "feel" right with the new outlooks we take on in our healing. Although our old behaviors failed to warm us, looked threadbare, and caused us to feel ashamed, we bring them out and wear them anyway because they are comfortable.

We want our new understandings reflected in our behavior. We want to permanently renounce denial and live in the truth. We want to be brave, cease to hide, and live to our potential. So when we find ourselves in our old coats, we get mad at ourselves.

Let us be patient with ourselves. The seductions of an old coat are real. In fact, we may need the comfort of an old coat, at least for a while, until we're ready to discard it permanently. Let's remind ourselves that habits and attitudes formed over a period of years won't disappear instantly simply because of new insights.

God is not impatient. God loves how bright and attractive we are in our new coats but understands and loves us in our tattered and torn ones as well.

God is not only fatherly.
God is also mother who lifts Her loved children
from the ground to her knee.
—Mechtilde of Magdeburg

Hiding Our Past

The woman admired a certain author and tuned into a TV program to watch him being interviewed. When she learned that the writer had survived a violent childhood, she was surprised. "He looked normal," she said, "but how could he be, when he's been so brutalized?"

The woman did not intend to be insensitive—maybe she had little experience with abuse—but words like hers make us, survivors of child abuse, nervous. We have worried obsessively about that very thing. Can we be normal? Despite our regular exteriors, aren't we hopelessly damaged inside?

We suspect that if people knew the truth about us they'd withhold their approval.

As children, we fretted that our families and living conditions would be exposed. We couldn't have been more embarrassed if we had been born with two heads. Now, as adults, we squirm when a conversation brings up "people with crazy backgrounds." No matter how capable we appear to ourselves in selected areas of our lives, we suspect that if people knew the truth about us they'd withhold their approval. So we don't mention the fact that we belong to a support group for survivors. We remain quiet when someone speaks about childhood abuse. If we confide an episode of abuse from our past, we watch for reactions, wondering if our listeners will reject us.

This kind of worry tells us something: we still don't get it. *The abuse was not our fault.* We did not deserve what we got, no matter what the abuser said. We don't have to be embarrassed for something that was outside our control. We can be angry, wistful, sad and baffled about our background. We can be embarrassed for our abusers, but we need not be embarrassed for ourselves.

We need to recognize that our background does not doom us. Many survivors go on to have rich, productive lives. Many great philanthropists, writers, humanitarians and reformers had abusive backgrounds, and the painful lessons they learned made them sensitive to the hurts of others.

We may not be ready to bless the terrible and unacceptable treatment we received as children, but we can acknowledge the strengths and sensitivities we developed and be grateful for them.

---

*"Believe in the light
so that you may become children of light."*
—John 12:36

❧

False Memory Coverage

When I read news stories about therapists who plant ideas of abuse in their clients' heads, or about someone who falsified a story about abuse, I get doubts about myself," the man admitted to his support group.

This middle-aged man had been rushing to a business appointment when a memory flashed into his head of a merciless beating by his father. He ended up hospitalized from the beating, a fact he later confirmed, and his body still bears the scars.

Denial has played such a role in our histories that it is easy for us to slip back into it.

Today the man feels uneasy when he reads about False Memory Syndrome. He realizes that a part of him doesn't want to believe in the beating. Also, his father had drummed into him that people would think him a liar if he told of the incident. As a result, the man worries about the validity and accuracy of his memory.

"How is it," the group's therapist pointed out, "that stories of therapists planting ideas of abuse into the minds of their clients, few in number, get so much publicity, and the many cases of verifiable repressed memory get little notice?" The therapist went on to mention that some leaders of the false-memory movement have themselves been convicted of abuse.

Denial has played such a role in our histories that it is easy for us to slip back into it. Believing that we are making the whole thing up can seem to offer a better alternative than recovering the truth we would prefer to forget.

Today let us have faith in ourselves and in the search for truth we are undertaking.

Faith is the bird that still sings
when the dawn is dark.
—Rabindranath Tagore

Favored Child, Unfavored Child

My dad hit me sometimes, but I was lucky. He really went after my brother," the woman said.

"I got punished more than my sister," another woman said. "The folks liked her better. So it's been easier for me to face our childhood than it has been for her, because she still feels she must be loyal to them."

In our "chin-up" way, we survivors of child abuse sometimes insist that either our pain or the resulting damage (or both) was less significant than the pain or damage our siblings suffered. *Caution:* this can be a form of denial, a way of staying away from the hurt and fear we felt as children or feel now.

> *Favored and unfavored children alike bring to adulthood distorted ideas about how love operates.*

True, one child in the family may endure most of the abuse while one or more children enjoy a favored status. In an abusive home, either role—

favored or unfavored—has difficulties associated with it.

The favored child suffers in watching her sibling's abuse, feels guilty that she is spared, and worries what will happen if she loses her preferred status. The out-of-favor child feels unloved, sad and indignant at the unfairness of the situation. Favored and unfavored children alike bring to adulthood distorted ideas about how love operates.

The roles we played in our original families give us our unique perceptions and ways of handling life today. Understandably, we may not want to trade places with our siblings. We must take care, however, that we don't use brave gratitude as a way to trivialize our pain or the resulting damage.

Let us acknowledge that the roles assigned to us in abusive families carried their individual challenges.

"You will know the truth,
and the truth will make you free."

—John 8:31

≈≈≈

Pain Is Never Trivial

As a child growing up in a fractured family, I assumed that most of my friends had normal and even wonderful lives. As an adult, however, I've become aware of how many children suffer tremendous pain within their families.

One night when my writing class wrote about anger, a woman read an account of how as a young child she had set out to surprise her mother by cleaning the bathroom. "This is trivial," she said to the group by way of introduction. She then told about how she had scoured the sink and tub, anticipating her mother's delight, and was in the middle of scrubbing the floor when her mother came home: "My mother yelled, 'How could you be so stupid! You've got soap all over!' I tried to explain to her that I wasn't finished yet, that I intended to rinse the floor. But she wouldn't listen."

"Worse things happen," the woman said with a shrug of her shoulders.

I told the woman I didn't agree that the incident was trivial.

Rather, I thought it sounded very painful.

"Worse things happen," the woman said with a shrug of her shoulders.

The man sitting next to her then read his piece. He told about fixing dinner for his little brother, putting the brother to bed, and trying to figure out how to run the washer so he could clean the stinking shirt he'd worn for a week. He moved living room furniture so that when his drunken parents came in they wouldn't stumble over anything. It was a heartbreaking account of childhood with two alcoholic parents.

Saying that we didn't have things so bad compared to others perpetuates our own patterns of denial.

Who had the most pain: the little girl whose hope of pleasing her mother died a cruel death or the little boy who had to parent himself and his little brother?

Why would we even ask that question? Yet that is how we trivialize our own pain. We say, "Others had it worse."

When misery comes, we suffer. Saying that we didn't have things so bad compared to others perpetuates our own patterns of denial. As children, we learned to deny our pain because it hurt too much to feel it or because our caretakers convinced us that denying or ignoring what we were feeling was the safest route: *If you keep crying, I'll give you something to cry about.*

Our hurts matter; they mattered when we were children, and they matter now. Part of our journey to health involves grieving the pain we were denied feeling and expressing in childhood.

Because of our hurts, we can understand the hurts of others. The man with alcoholic parents wore a look of deep compassion as he listened to the woman read her piece about cleaning the bathroom to surprise her mother.

We don't have to pretend anymore. We don't have to apologize with, "Others had it worse." We can acknowledge our individual pain.

The light shines in the darkness,
and the darkness did not overcome it.

—John 1:5

~

Loving Our Bodies

One day it came to me," the woman said. "What I'd called my hyper-modesty was actually shame."

Abuse violates the body of a child. In sexual abuse this is patently obvious, but physical abuse and verbal abuse also trespass on the sanctity of the body, wounding our perception of ourselves.

"My father looked at me in disgust," one woman remembers, "when I walked past in my nightgown. He said I was revolting because I was too fat." For years, this woman has struggled with her body image.

As children, we felt helpless to refute the ideas caretakers conveyed to us about our bodies.

A man told this story: "When I was six, I got out of the tub with an erection. My dad saw it, left the bathroom, and came back with a butcher knife. He said he was going to cut off my penis, and I believed him. Then after a minute he stopped and said, 'If you ever touch yourself again, I *will* cut it off.'" Years later the man found himself in counseling over sexual issues.

Those of us who are survivors of child abuse received early messages that may explain why we are hyper-modest or overly seductive. We may fail to set good boundaries for our bodies regarding inappropriate touching, and we may attract spouses and partners who further abuse our bodies. Eating disorders, from obesity to anorexia, sometimes can be traced to abuse. Discomfort with sex on the one hand, or sexual addiction on the other, can have roots in abuse.

"I'm not going to blame abuse for my lack of willpower in the way I eat," we may object. And while it's true that we want to take responsibility for ourselves in the present, we must remember that looking back at how we formed ideas about our bodies may be therapeutic. As children, we felt helpless to refute the ideas caretakers conveyed to us about our bodies. Now, we are no longer helpless.

Let us resolve to find joy in our splendid bodies: the intricate mechanism of our skin, the magnificence of our throbbing hearts, the awesome power of our brains, the complex working of our hands, eyes and olfactory system. We are, in Shakespeare's words, "a piece of work...infinite in faculties, in form and moving."

Our body is precious. It is a vehicle for awakening.
Treat it with care.

—The Buddha

Patience with Progress

I'm sick of looking at this," I told a friend.

At a weekend seminar, I found myself working on an issue of childhood abuse. Others, I believed, were working on present-day goals, but there I sat, stomach tight, eyes swimming, filling my notebook with thoughts about abuse.

When I saw the seminar leader sitting alone, I decided to ask him for help. After explaining to him how much I wanted to move on to other things, he asked, "Why? If you're not finished with this, why would you want to move on?"

"If you're not finished with this, why would you want to move on?"

When we get sick and tired of working on healing, we may at times set for ourselves an artificial timetable. "By June, I'll be healed and will then get on with my life." "This will be the last support group I join." "I'll finish with counseling before Christmas." Expectations about how long we need for healing set us up for frustration.

We may not fully realize the depth of our pain. It may be less or greater than someone else's. We can't predict when we'll be done with our work. A mended bone still hurts when it rains, and our emotional pain can work the same way.

Digging to the bottom of pain takes time, and many variables affect the rate of our progress. Those of us who didn't admit to the extent of our abuse when we started recovery and healing, for example, may actually need more time. Regular contact with our abusers, or no contact whatsoever with them, may hasten or delay healing. Plus, the frequency and quality of interactions with family and friends will directly affect our progress.

"Why would you want to move beyond this if you're not finished?" the trainer asked that day. I returned to my seat, reconciled to work on what I needed to accomplish.

Our progress comes sometimes in leaps, sometimes in baby steps. Let us trust that our healing is monumental, even when it seems slow.

When I sit in darkness,
the Lord will be a light to me.

—Micah 7:8

Taking Back Our Lives

Shedding Old Skin

You can't teach an old dog new tricks."

"The leopard can't change his spots."

We desire changes in ourselves, but popular sayings like these can hold us back. Concerned that we may have been permanently marked by our abuse, we look at other people and wonder if anyone ever really changes. We question whether the work and attention needed for healing can be worth the sometimes long and painful effort.

We can shed all the old skin that doesn't reflect the glory of our real selves.

As a matter of truth, old dogs can and do learn new tricks; canine trainers demonstrate this repeatedly. And, indeed, a leopard's spots do change in shape and color over the course of the animal's life.

Let's consider another creature that gives us a more evident demonstration of change: the snake.

The snake sheds an old skin that no longer fits and slithers off in a new one that better suits it.

We are working to cast off damaged, careworn skin. The innermost part of us was and remains beautiful, a magnificent creation of love. We can shed all the old skin that doesn't reflect the glory of our real selves.

We are healing. We are casting off what doesn't fit anymore. Soon, and very soon, we will be sunning ourselves on a warm rock, wearing a bright new skin that reflects more closely who we really are.

"For nothing will be impossible with God."

—Luke 1:37

Being Adult

The evening ahead looked difficult; I needed to have a frank conversation with someone, and I worried that the exchange would strain our relationship. The part of me that fears conflict switched on worst-case imaginings, and my stomach began to hurt.

"What are you wearing?" a friend asked.

"Overalls," I said.

"How about wearing your most adult outfit?" she suggested. "Also, put your car keys in your pocket. When feelings of being small and helpless come up tonight, touch the keys as a reminder that you are now an adult and you can get in the car and drive away from a situation you don't like. You know how to find safety."

We can respect what is going on inside us and deal with ourselves gently.

I took my friend's advice. I wore a stylish but comfortable outfit, and I put my car keys in a convenient pocket where I could easily find them. Throughout the evening, I often repeated to myself that I was a mature, capable person who could voice her concerns. Every time I felt anxiety over the pending confrontation, I reached for the keys and let them remind me of the prerogatives of being adult.

The evening held no actual threat for me; the difficult conversation took place in a public setting. But my younger, emotional self had been trained to say, "You ask the wrong question and you'll be sorry."

If we survivors of childhood abuse sometimes feel small and powerless, we don't need to scold ourselves or feel absurd. Rather, we can respect what is going on inside us and deal with ourselves gently. We can use crutches when we need them, to get through times that look difficult.

A friend of mine uses a visualizing trick of taking her scared inner child on her lap and comforting her. Another friend entrusts her younger self into the keeping of a kind, deceased relative before heading off on a challenging task.

We can employ whatever devices we need to remain adult in the face of situations that trigger childlike reactions. That does not mean we are childish. Quite the contrary. Admitting our fears, finding formulas to deal with them, and figuring out new behaviors is the mature response.

When Jesus saw him lying there
and knew that he had been there a long time,
he said to him, "Do you want to be made well?"
—John 5:6

Taking Back Our Lives

Giving Ourselves Approval

No matter how old we are, those of us who have survived child abuse often find ourselves hungering for the approval of our parents. Even if we are parents ourselves, or taking care of those same aging parents, we still yearn for the affirmation we did not receive as children.

This hunger for parental approval often displays itself as a sense of feeling unfulfilled after achieving a difficult personal goal. We begin to wonder if the results were worth the effort, since we feel a void we can't explain. This need for approval may also manifest itself in our tendency to be overachievers, underachievers or perfectionists.

When we were growing up, gaining the approval of our caretakers was tricky.

When we were growing up, gaining the approval of our caretakers was tricky. Some of us were coerced into unhealthy activities to gain approval. Some of us got lavish praise one minute and harsh disapproval the next, leaving us confused about how to please others.

So we come to adulthood obsessive about gaining approval or convinced we cannot gain it at all. It may be years since we had those painful experiences, yet we still know a hollow place within that craves affirmation from those who withheld it. A fifty-year-old attorney with a brilliant record of courtroom wins admits sadly, "I know that my mother will never feel proud of me."

We must challenge the sadness that comes from yearning for acknowledgment. We can and must give to ourselves the approval we want. We ourselves can take note of our own good qualities and appreciate our own admirable actions that have positive effects on others. We can bask in those moments when we feel proud of our behavior.

If we still don't feel like we measure up, we can ask a supportive person for reassurance. If that seems risky, we can seek the same thing in meditation or prayer.

You are a child of the universe,
no less than the trees and the stars;
you have a right to be here.

—Max Ehrmann

Two People at Once

A t times, our behavior seems to lag far behind our new-found understanding. We know, for example, what situations make us feel fearful, angry or helpless. We may have made a decision to change our thinking and behavior. Perhaps we have a strong selection of affirmations to review and actions to take to modify our behavior. We may even understand that we are now safe, no longer powerless. Yet too often we watch ourselves fall into old patterns and react to old triggers.

We acquired our thinking patterns when we were impressionable.

We mean to behave as mature adults, but we find ourselves acting in unhealthy ways, leaving us feeling disappointed and worried. Maybe we haven't learned much after all?

We acquired our thinking patterns when we were impressionable. That doesn't mean we are condemned to live by those same patterns the rest of our lives. It does mean, however, that the patterns are strong and extremely familiar. Thus it isn't at all unusual to experience ourselves as a former person and a new person, simultaneously residing in one body. As we succeed in practicing new ways of behaving, the former person will hold less and less sway.

Let us practice patience with ourselves. Let us understand our history and our struggles, and let us be compassionate when our unhealed self governs our behavior. And when we see ourselves operating in new and healthy ways, let us be quick to give ourselves full credit in the form of lavish self-praise.

Your vision will become clear
only when you look into your own heart.
Who looks outside, dreams;
who looks inside, awakes.

—Carl Jung

Becoming Authentic

earching for truth will force us to look with honesty at the pain we suffered in childhood. But we may not be able to stop there. We may find that we've brought our old habit of denial into adulthood.

As children we became experts at not seeing, at becoming numb, at not feeling (or at least at denying what we were feeling). Although we may have raged at our treatment, we learned to ignore the wounds and the injustice, living instead in a fantasy world and looking for ways to control our environment to make it tolerable. We may even have made excuses for our caretakers.

Today, as adults, that denial lingers deep within.

Those of us with religious upbringings found rationales for not being real. We told ourselves we were being "good" little children. We acted as peacemakers. We put others before ourselves. We defused conflict. The only trouble was that our resentments boiled unresolved underneath.

Today, as adults, that denial lingers deep within. If we feel scared, we tell ourselves we're being silly or that we lack faith.

If someone challenges our opinion, we quickly decide we're probably wrong. We repudiate our assets and talents, afraid we'll attract attention because, in the past, attention could mean pain.

But now the Spirit of Truth whispers to us to become authentic. We can acknowledge our own experiences and thoughts, even the negative ones. We can start valuing ourselves by respecting and taking seriously our feelings, opinions and abilities.

Today God wants us to listen for and honor the messages we get from our deepest, authentic selves.

In this life we are to become heaven
so that God might find a home here.

—Meister Eckhart

Taking Back Our Lives

The Inevitability of Growth

There are days when the change we desire seems to elude us. We search for examples of progress and can't find them. We wonder: What if I've done it all wrong? What if I slip back, all the way back? What if my hard trek uphill, toward the crest of healthy living, has been for nothing?

At such times, it is important for us to have faith in the process. We have planted the seeds, watered them and provided a sheltering environment. Now our flowering will obey laws of nature. A seed in the ground doesn't need every spring day to be fair and warm for it to burst open and begin to push up from the soil. Rather, it needs only a certain number of days to be sunny.

We can trust that a friendly Providence is assisting us.

The flower couldn't decide not to grow; it can't change its mind and decide to remain a seed. If conditions are right, it simply grows.

It is not necessary that every one of our actions be perfect. We can trust that a friendly Providence is assisting us. Even on those days when no warmth seems to be shining on our emerging selves, development is taking place. Old habits of thinking and behaving may tempt us to be hard on ourselves or believe we are alone in our struggle. But that isn't true. We can put aside our self-doubt, knowing that God supports our aspirations for wholeness. Our growth doesn't depend solely, or even primarily, on our own efforts.

We have turned our faces toward the sun. Even on rainy days, the sun is there, radiating goodwill on our intended growth.

Forgetting what lies behind
and straining forward to what lies ahead,
I press on.

—Philippians 3:13

Rolling with Mistakes

Some of us take our mistakes in stride, dust ourselves off when we fall, and move on with confidence intact.

Others of us agonize over our mistakes, replay them in our minds, go over what we should have done, enlarge the consequences of our errors, and scold, scold, scold ourselves. If it is our practice to be hard on ourselves, we take the entire blame for a situation on our own shoulders, forgetting that others may have played a role as well. Then, tiring of being entirely at fault, we change our minds and decide that others were entirely wrong, that we bear very little responsibility.

We do not have to prolong our victimization by victimizing ourselves.

Wouldn't we live more peacefully if we accepted our humanity and forgave ourselves readily? Would that not allow us to ease up on others too?

We survivors of child abuse grew up with a strong sense of shame. We lacked the maturity and judgment to see that the episodes of abuse we encountered were not our fault.

Sexual abuse survivors often have an especially strong sense of shame and wrongness, which their abusers may have helped to plant in them: "Uncle Bob wouldn't have to do this if you weren't such a pretty little girl." "I knew you wanted this and that's why I followed you here." "I bought you the things you wanted; now you can make me happy."

We do not have to prolong our victimization by victimizing ourselves. We must stop feeling guilty for events that weren't our fault and stop berating ourselves for present mistakes.

In the aftermath of a mistake, we can wish that we had behaved differently. We can think about how we might handle things differently in the future. We can offer apologies when appropriate. Then we can go on, heads held high, into our day.

---

*God saw everything he had made
and indeed, it was very good.*

—Genesis 1:31

Saying Yes to Plenty

If God, like my caretakers, is apt to take away what is precious to me, I'll simply take it away from myself before I get it. If I block myself from getting what I want, then I won't have to endure the pain of losing it." This thinking seems so irrational that I have a hard time admitting that I do it. So let me check it out with the facts of my life.

Do I have the financial security I want?

Do I have the depth in relationships I want?

Do I confidently embrace the good things I experience?

If the answer to any of these questions is "no," then it might be a hint that I am refusing to allow positive things into my life.

Abused children learn how much it hurts to become attached.

Abused children learn how much it hurts to become attached. At a subconscious—perhaps even conscious—level, we remember our losses. We lost safety, innocence, homes, pets. Now, as adults, we watch tangible and intangible things elude our grasp, even though we appear to be working hard to gain them. This is also true in our experience of religious faith. Because our care-takers took from us what wasn't theirs to take, we assume that God acts the same way and thereby lose the warmth of a secure faith that could be ours.

But through conscious effort, we can change the belief that all good things will either elude us or be taken from us. We can bring our fears to the light, look at them without judgment and put new beliefs in their place. We can say yes to plenty. We can meditate, pray and listen for answers, knowing that God wants to replace our anxiety and insecurity with reassuring truth.

"I came that they may have life,
and have it abundantly."

—John 10:10

Correcting Body Images

The slender woman with flowing blond hair huddled in the corner, a towel wrapped around her torso. "I look awful in a swimsuit," she moaned. "My stomach pooches out."

A teenage girl beside her waited until the motel pool emptied before she removed her towel. She complained about having flabby legs.

A third woman in the group, an athletic brunette, complained that she was too muscular.

The three women looked beautiful to the friends who overheard them. But they had magnified what they saw as flaws until they could scarcely let themselves be seen in swimsuits at a pool.

We grew up to be ashamed of our physical selves.

Body issues afflict our culture in general, leaving few of us feeling unqualified pride in our physical appearance. For some of us, the abuse we suffered as children exacerbates the problem today, because the abuse violated the sanctity of our young bodies. We grew up to be ashamed of our physical selves.

Sexually abused survivors often grow up to be either sexually overactive or numb, but not content. Sexually abused children who were told that they brought the violation on themselves because they were so cute will likely fear being attractive adults. This type of abuse during childhood can lead to survivors being overweight, underweight, or suffering from eating disorders.

Survivors of physical battering can scarcely love the body that withstood so much pain. We may be inattentive to physical health and anesthetized to physical symptoms. Emotional insults, too, can be insidious, leaving us too wounded to care for our appearance.

As adults, we don't need to discount and dishonor our bodies—verbally or physically—the way others did. Rather, we can choose to value them. We can treat them well, give them rest and keep them healthy through good nutrition and appropriate exercise. Our bodies need not be perfect for us to honor and esteem them, and we can start right now.

Today I will have reverence for the splendid body that houses my soul.

There is no wealth better than health of body.
—Sirach 30:16

Healthy Motives

Maybe we've won a reputation for being helpful and generous. Maybe we've gone the extra mile in relationships and put the needs of others before our own. Then one day on our journey toward healing, we come to the disappointing realization that we've been helpful for the wrong reasons. We were scared. We believed ourselves unworthy. We wanted to curry favor with our loved ones and with God. We wanted to look good in the eyes of others.

Survivors of child abuse often have strong sensitivities to the needs and reactions of other people. As children, we had to; that was one way we survived. So as adults, we keep discerning the moods and desires of others, finding ways to make ourselves significant in their eyes and in our own.

When we responsibly consider our own needs, are we being selfish?

When we give up fear, do we become insensitive to others? No. When we responsibly consider our own needs, are we being selfish? No. Our ability to read people and detect their moods and needs will stay with us as a useful gift, but we can start behaving in caring ways out of different motives.

In our new health, we may still be generous or self-sacrificing, but not because we feel undeserving or because God did not intend for us to have nice things or because we need to improve our image with God and our neighbors. Rather, we will give of ourselves because the experience of generosity rewards and expands us. Connecting with fellow travelers on the journey helps us to be fully alive.

This is astonishing—we strip away our egos,
empty ourselves of our very selves,
and then take in Christ, holiness and bliss.

—Meister Eckhart

Taking Back Our Lives

Standing Tall

At one group counseling session I attended, an unusually tall woman named Julie asked for hugs from the rest of us, and we all lined up to embrace our stately sister. But when Julie bent over to hug the counselor, the counselor said, "Stand up, Julie. Let me hug you tall."

Julie laughed. "But you won't be able to reach me."

The counselor said with confidence, "Oh, but I will."

I found myself feeling tearful. How often have I done that very thing—made myself small for someone else's comfort? Although I don't have impressive physical stature like Julie, I have areas of talent, skill and intelligence in which I am tall. Yet I've often crouched, ducked and shrunk to make myself less noticeable. I wanted to be pleasing and unthreatening. As a child, being inconspicuous became important to my survival.

As a child, being inconspicuous became important to my survival.

We survivors of child abuse are tall now, and we are ready to put away childish things. We can answer the call to stand proud, to be as grand as we really are. It doesn't serve the world for us to sell ourselves short. If others have to stretch to reach us, isn't that good for them too?

God, our loving supporter, smiles on our magnificence. God wants us to be as tall as we are capable of being.

"Rejoice with me,
for I have found my sheep that was lost."

—Luke 15:6

≋

Cutting Ourselves Slack

File folders and stacks of paper hid the top of my kitchen table. It was April 13, and I knew I'd be up late the next two nights doing my taxes.

When I read the instructions on one form, I grew discouraged. When I read another set of instructions, I felt panic. By the third set of instructions, I was despondent.

I made myself a cup of hot tea and tried to get a grip, remembering that millions of people do tax returns every year. But I simply could not stop feeling overwhelmed and unhappy.

When we find a routine or distasteful job throwing us for a loop, we might not notice what else is going on.

Two days later, with everything organized and totals calculated, I transferred figures to the final form. With effort and perseverance, I had tackled my complicated tax situation, waded through receipts and called for help when I needed it. As I signed my returns, I felt buoyant.

Is a tax form a mental stretch for me? No. Am I capable of

reading forms and doing sums? Of course. So why did I get so scared?

When we find a routine or distasteful job throwing us for a loop, we might not notice what else is going on. For survivors of child abuse, the answer often lies in the past. It was dangerous to make a mistake. Our efforts won us humiliation, physical pain, maybe even torture. "Just do your best and that will be fine" was not the message we heard.

Now we can be gentle with ourselves. The adult we are today can acknowledge and respect the fear and insecurity of our youth. Then, with gentle attention, that same adult can offer the younger self the reassurance we all need: "I know you're scared, but you're safe now."

A counselor and child abuse survivor told me that when she first started doing public speaking she would become so terrified that she would tremble and get nauseated. To help steady herself, she would talk to the young and frightened child she once was. "I began to tell my little person, 'You don't have to do this. You stay here, or hold onto my skirt and hide, and I'll go out there and speak.' It worked."

Let us find creative ways to be kind to ourselves and make stressful situations less threatening.

He will cover you with his pinions,
and under his wings you will find refuge.
—Psalm 91:4

Needing and Finding Validation

We survivors of child abuse doubt our memories.

A chance remark such as "Your dad is such a nice guy" can throw us into confusion, because we remember Dad as the guy who punched us in the face (or whatever). We begin to doubt ourselves, our memories, our reality.

"Maybe Dad and I just clashed."

"I probably asked for it. I was a rowdy kid."

"I guess Dad did a lot of good. He was my Boy Scout leader."

If only we had videos of the ugly scenes that took place. Then we could see how it really was: we were kids, they were adults. We did not have equal responsibility in the episodes of abuse.

We can be further confused in our memories because abusers know how to show a good face to the world. They can be charming and glib, manipulative and canny.

We probably won't ever get the snapshot or video that

would convince us of the abuser's wrongdoing, but we can learn to respect the validation we get from our own insides.

For example, a woman who is extremely phobic about knives is surprised that her children aren't afraid of knives as well. "When I get out a knife to make a salad or something, I think I ought to assure my children that the knife is not dangerous when properly used. But then I notice that they aren't even paying attention." The fact that her children felt comfortable around knives made her suspect that her own apprehension was unnatural. She also realized that her fear had a basis in what had happened to her as a child, when she had been repeatedly threatened with a knife.

> By respecting that which triggers our fears, we validate our own experiences. We also can open ourselves to validation from others.

By respecting that which triggers our fears, we validate our own experiences. We also can open ourselves to validation from others. Many of us find that when we are ready such validation comes from other people simply because we start being more truthful in our conversations, giving others permission to do likewise. In the case of the woman with the knife, her husband was able to point out to her that her fear of knives was not irrational, given what had happened to her as a child.

We came to adulthood with an outlook that our *very being* is wrong or that we are, at the very least, *in the wrong* much of the time. So it has been hard for us to trust our memories

Taking Back Our Lives

and impressions. However, if we learn to be open to the truth of our past we can get the support we need from within ourselves or from the perceptions of others.

"The kingdom of God has come near to you."

—Luke 10:9

≈≈

Writing Our Pain

The most powerful writing I see from students in my creative writing classes happens on the night I ask them to write about an unresolved anger or painful episode from childhood. Before this exercise, I strongly encourage the students to reach for raw, childhood feelings. "For these few minutes, don't view the episode or situation with adult forgiveness and perspective. Don't coat feelings with mature understanding. Children feel wounds keenly, and we're trying to reach powerful feelings we can mine for writing."

The exercise isn't therapy, I tell them, but it may be therapeutic. Rather, it aims to show students how evocative writing can be when it touches bare feelings.

Through writing, we can touch feelings and truths deep within ourselves.

When students read their pieces, their voices crack and sometimes tears run down their cheeks. Once or twice, students have run from the room because they were ill. One woman left the class and didn't return at all that evening. The woman later told me that she'd sought counseling because of what she wrote.

This writing usually rings with vivid language and commanding emotion, so when students read their pieces, the rest of us scarcely breathe. Sometimes, when a student finishes reading, spontaneous applause follows, as classmates respond to the honest emotion they've heard.

This exercise illustrates how useful writing can be in our process of healing. Through writing, we can touch feelings and truths deep within ourselves. Our brains often swirl with confusion and conflicting messages, but when we pick up a pen or sit down at a computer and pour out thoughts and emotions we sometimes calm the turmoil.

Don't worry about creating beautiful literary prose. Simply make your writing beautiful in its truthfulness.

I write entirely to find out what I'm thinking.

—Joan Didion

Acceptance versus Resignation

"I wanted this job/relationship/deal/vacation/weekend/afternoon to work out a different way. But (sigh), it's okay. I practice acceptance these days."

Is this acceptance, or is it resignation?

As abused children we learned to cope, to make do, to be inconspicuous, to lower our expectations and standards, to settle for little or nothing. We did what we needed to do for survival and became proficient at it.

> We did what we needed to do for survival.

Today it takes insight and honesty for us to see the difference between acceptance and resignation. An ability to let go of outcomes, trusting that God and the universe work to ensure our benefit at all times, is one thing. Swallowing disappointment, anger and sadness or surrendering to hopelessness is quite another.

We may mouth identical words whether we are practicing acceptance or resignation, but there are differences that we can know, that we can feel.

Acceptance feels peaceful. It quiets our bellies and calms our souls. It allows us to go on with hope. It gives us power.

Resignation feels uneasy, fatiguing. It feels like defeat. It encourages us to stay in the same place.

How can we recognize whether we are exercising acceptance or resignation? We can be quiet and listen to our insides. If we are falling into resignation, we can admit it and be gentle with ourselves. As we heal, however, more and more we will observe ourselves practicing genuine acceptance.

Our inner nature is being renewed day by day.
—2 Corinthians 4:16

Leaving Behind a
Make-Believe World

hildren in abusive homes learn to live inside a fairy tale. As a child I believed that someday my parents would love me in the way I wanted to be loved—if I could just get it right, if I could just accumulate the right kind of achievements, if I could just get a deadly disease, if I could just save a drowning child.

I practiced the scene where they would recognize my worth, when they would look at me with fondness and say, "I won't harm or abandon you ever again."

All we have is the present, and we can make this a safe and rewarding life.

Sometimes, even as adults, we believe that this moment may yet come—maybe when we confront our abusers with the truth and make them see how they hurt us or failed to protect us.

Don't count on it. Our abusers did not support our growth when we were young; most likely they will not begin to support our movement toward health now. The truth can be upsetting for them.

It is too late for us to be our parents' cherished children; the childhood we yearned for eluded us. All we have is the present, and we can make this a safe and rewarding life. We can take care of ourselves the way we wished our parents had. We can take ourselves to the zoo, buy ourselves a locket, find pictures in clouds.

God stands ready to be our limitless source, better than any parent of our fantasy. We can square our shoulders and affirm ourselves as cherished children of God. Looking back, we find evidence of the Divine in our survival. When we open our eyes we find evidence of the Spirit in our present journey toward healing.

Then Jesus said to him,
"What do you want me to do for you?"
The blind man said to him,
"My teacher, let me see again."

—Mark 10:51

Stating Our Feelings

Because I learned to conceal hurt at an early age, one of the hardest things for me to say to someone is, "What you said and did hurt my feelings." In fact, as a child I was so good at hiding hurt that I hid it from myself. I often didn't know *what* I was feeling. Even after I became aware of hurt feelings, it would take me a long time to believe that anyone would care. So why say anything?

My squinting into the truth, even though it hurt, was worth the effort.

Learning to express hurt feelings can be like trying to adjust to daylight after spending time in a cave. We want to open our eyes to see, but the bright sunlight is painful. We have to squint, opening our eyes little by little, until we can finally face the full light of day. Since I started speaking up when I feel hurt, there have been times when the response was less than satisfying, when the bright light of my honesty brought only more pain. One person told me I didn't need to be so sensitive; another tried to talk me out of what I felt. But even at those awkward times, I felt better and more powerful for having expressed myself. My squinting into the truth, even though it hurt, was worth the effort.

At other times, saying the words "I feel hurt" has produced almost magical results. The other person listened and my statement led to a useful discussion. Our relationship deepened, and I rid myself of a festering resentment.

Recognizing when we feel hurt and telling the other person about that feeling can be a constructive step in getting comfortable with, and then becoming appreciative of, our feelings.

Since then, we have such a hope,
we act with great boldness.
—2 Corinthians 3:12

Taking Back Our Lives

Wobbly but Full of Promise

I experienced a stressful family situation one weekend, and my awkward reaction to it made me question whether I'd made any significant progress in my healing from childhood abuse.

A friend tried to reassure me. "You've only recently pecked out of your shell," she said, "so you're a little wet and sort of wobbly. It may be that you're a bit strange looking right now, but given time to dry off you'll be fluffy and cute. Before long, you'll be soaring, and your family will see how graceful you are."

If only the world would hold still while we test our legs and wings.

We all love metaphors about hatching new life and eventual flight. We love them for their truth. Such metaphors are helpful in our healing.

We may feel wobbly with our new selves. If only the world would hold still while we test our legs and wings. But disappointments, health issues and strained relationships ask for our attention, and we may have little energy for such things.

This stressful family situation gave me the opportunity to experiment with being a "new" me in the midst of a group of people who were used to the "old" me. When the new me did not behave perfectly by my standards, I was deeply disappointed in myself. "I wanted to be a strong, brave person in that circumstance," I told my friend. "Instead, I sank into guilt and doubt."

We survivors of child abuse have powerful conditioning that says we must not mess up. Today let us put that view behind us. Know instead that it is all right to be unsteady as we try out shaky new legs and wings. When we disappoint others or even ourselves, let us applaud our effort and commitment, whether we come off as brave or scared, confident or timid, ludicrous or magnificent.

"Nor will they say, 'Look here it is!' or 'There it is!'
For, in fact, the kingdom of God is within you."
—Luke 17:21

❧❧

Respecting Our Own Needs

Fear, insecurity and feelings of unworthiness make us reluctant to ask for what we want.

As abused children we seldom got what we wanted and often didn't get the basic things we absolutely needed. Even the fundamental need for safety wasn't always met. When we made a request or asserted a right, it sometimes brought painful results. So as children we learned to conceal our needs and wants from people. Even today we sometimes operate out of the hope that others will see what we need, rather than letting them know.

Our wishes and needs count, and we can ask to have them met.

A friend, the mother of a toddler, wanted more help from her husband and in-laws when her baby was born, but she didn't ask for it. "I thought it was obvious I was drowning," she says. "A ship appeared on the horizon, and when I saw it coming, I knew it would pick me up. Still, I didn't call out or say I needed help, and the ship sailed past. Then I realized it wasn't a rescue vessel after all. It was a sightseeing boat."

My friend also admitted that if she had just called for help, the passengers on that sightseeing boat would have responded.

Our wishes and needs count, and we can ask to have them met. We are no longer in danger. If we are, we can move to change that situation. When we first begin to present our wants and needs, however, we may experience fears similar to the ones we knew during childhood: our stomachs may churn, our shoulders may tighten, our eyes may sting with tears. We must be ready for these reactions and not let them hinder our asking.

Nor can we force anyone to help us, and we don't need to stipulate what form the help should take. Sometimes we'll be frustrated because people will disappoint or refuse us. But we can and must ask. Often, people of goodwill may be pleased to help.

Today let us affirm that our wants and needs matter, and that we can make them known.

My false and private self is the one who wants to exist
outside the reach of God's will and God's love—
outside of reality and outside of life.
And such a self cannot but help be an illusion.
                                        —Thomas Merton

Healing for Ourselves and for Others

Our healing from child abuse is not for ourselves alone. As we become more whole we deal with others in healthier ways, and that is good for them.

But what if those around us don't like the changes? We're putting so much energy into getting healthier and stronger that we don't want to exert additional energy defending our new behaviors as well.

Even people who support our journey to health may fear our changes.

Yet the experiences of those who are healing tell us that new ways of thinking and behaving can threaten family members, spouses and close friends. Before we started healing, these people knew how we would act and speak. Now, when we behave in different ways, we throw the familiar social system out of kilter. We may have played scapegoat, wimp or meanie, and people may not have liked us in those roles; but they may feel equally uneasy with our new faces of confidence and honesty.

Even people who support our journey to health may fear our changes as destabilizing and rejecting. They may test our love and try to maneuver us into old ways of behaving. It can be difficult for us to hold our own and not slide backwards.

We can be understanding and demonstrate continuing love for these important people, all the while forging ahead on our healing path. As healed persons, we have more to offer everyone.

When I am whole, I contribute more to the health of my family, neighborhood, nation and planet.

Lord, make me an instrument of your peace.
—Francis of Assisi

Embracing Pain

A friend of mine longed to take ballet lessons when she was a child. But her first real opportunity to study ballet didn't come until after she graduated from college. After a time she progressed enough that she could buy her first pair of pointe shoes. They made her feet miserable. Much of the time, bloody, raw blisters covered her toes.

"My feet bled a lot," my friend said, "and the bones in my feet were so sore that I could hardly walk. But I'd never been happier."

In the past, we often were helpless against the pain that was aimed our way. Therefore as adults we can, and often do, go to great lengths to avoid pain, seeing all pain as negative.

Pain can be part of something good.

But pain can be part of something good. Facing the abuse we experienced will, in most cases, bring us pain. But we freely and willingly choose this pain because we know it will bring us to wholeness. The pain *is* for something, just as learning to dance on pointe had the outcome my friend desired, despite the pain it caused.

We are no longer helpless. If pain is not being imposed on us from without, then it is ours to embrace. Yes, the work of recovering from abuse may cause our hearts to bleed and give us raw blisters on our feelings, but in time we will be restored and healed. We will dance then, in ways we've always dreamed about.

Let us run with perseverance
the race that is set before us.

—Hebrews 12:1

Taking Back Our Lives

A True Self-Picture

When I show my supervisor a project," the man said, "she criticizes it and I feel disappointed. But when I show it around to my coworkers they praise my efforts and I feel better."

We survivors of child abuse had no range of feedback when we were young. Particularly as young children, we had limited contact outside our families. If our families told us in words or actions that we were stupid, unlovable, worthless, too much trouble or undeserving, we had little opportunity to seek second opinions that might dilute those hurtful views. Is it any wonder that those sick ideas had power over us? Our caretakers loomed as gods, and who were we to question their opinions?

We can see God as dependable, trustworthy and (dare we say it?) proud of us.

But we can repudiate those opinions now. Meditation, study, counseling, support groups and friendships can impart to us a true picture of ourselves.

We who may have created the deity in our caretakers' image

also need to seek a truer view of God. Healed, we can view ourselves as worthy, lovable and deserving. We can likewise see God as dependable, trustworthy and (dare we say it?) proud of us.

And finally, seeing ourselves as magnificent will open our eyes to the magnificence of others.

The day of my spiritual awakening
was the day that I saw—and knew I saw—
all things in God
and God in all things.
—Mechtilde of Magdeburg

Casting a Worry Net

Life held uncertainties for us as abused children, and we learned to worry.

That habit likely has followed us into adulthood. Does an unexpected bill come in? This may be the start of a financial downslide that ends in economic collapse. Does the doctor hesitate when we ask a question? Maybe he doesn't want to say what is really wrong, and wouldn't losing our health be disastrous for the people depending on us? Do we notice a cooling in a friendship? How lonely it would be if we lost this particular friend. And then it probably will be only a matter of time until other friends disappear as well.

The spiral of worry continues, but we can call a halt to it.

The spiral of worry continues, but we can call a halt to it. It may be one of the most difficult changes we undertake, but we can stem this flow of anxious thoughts.

A woman in a support group shared this strategy: she casts a "worry net." She decides how far she wants to cast it: into the next month, the next year, the next five years. Then she refuses to allow worried imaginings to stray beyond that net's reach. She says that this little exercise helps limit the reach and power of her fears.

With time and practice, our worry nets need not be thrown far. We can cast our nets shorter and shorter distances. When we become truly skilled, we will cast our worry nets ahead just a day or two at a time.

Even people with stable underpinnings can't know their futures. Those of us who never learned to trust the future can keep in mind that we have come through difficulties before and will successfully come through any troubles that arise now.

"Consider the lilies of the field, how they grow;
they neither toil nor spin.
Yet I tell you, even Solomon in all his glory
was not clothed like one of these.
But if God so clothes the grass of the field,
which is alive today and tomorrow is thrown into the oven,
will he not much more clothe you—you of little faith?"
—Matthew 6:28–30

Taking Back Our Lives

Choosing the Best

It's as if someone offers us a choice: a sumptuous dinner on a china plate prepared by the world's greatest chef or a peanut butter sandwich on a paper plate. We survivors of child abuse say, "I'll just have the peanut butter, thank you."

If we didn't let ourselves have even the peanut butter, we'd look like terrible martyrs. So we take the sandwich and the rationales that go with it. "Peanut butter is very nourishing and economical." (Practical.) "If everyone in the world can't have an elegant meal, I shouldn't either." (Altruistic.) "I will have the sumptuous meal someday, but for now, the peanut butter will do." (Waiting until I earn it.)

We must remember: things are different now.

Why do we pass up the sumptuous? Maybe in the past we've reached out for it and had our hands slapped. Maybe we thought we'd like it too much and then it would be taken away, like so many other things that were lost to us.

We must remember: things are different now. We are no

longer helpless children who can't let ourselves want good things and enjoy good things. We can hunger for it all, enjoy it all: safety, trust, love, acceptance.

Yes, we can allow ourselves to settle at times for peanut butter for worthwhile and important reasons. But we can also rejoice when we reach for and enjoy the best. No slaps this time, no tricks from threatening and criticizing sources. Rather, just our own healthy and strong judgment in the moment. Just the finest, the greatest, the highest good for us.

It is time for us to live richly.

"For I have seen God face to face,
yet my life is preserved."

—Genesis 32:30

Taking Back Our Lives

Reveling in the Goodness of Today

The sun hangs in a cobalt sky, a rainbow hovers on the horizon and flowers bloom beside the sidewalks. We breathe in the freshness of the air, but we do it cautiously, keeping one eye trained over our shoulder. What will happen to take this moment from us? What sour event will change things? Is life winding up to slap us?

As abused children, we made an observation: good times don't last. Now, anxious about what may be coming along to hurt us, we don't fully savor our safe, harmonious moments.

We aren't helpless anymore.

But something has changed since we were young and had little control over painful situations. We aren't helpless anymore. We have grown up to be people who can work out solutions for ourselves. We can find safety and support when we need it. Groups, agencies, therapists and trusted friends stand ready to help us. If we're grappling with vague, nameless dangers, we can stop, talk to ourselves and change our thinking. If someone actually takes steps to harm us, we are now able to turn to the law if need be to protect ourselves.

We no longer need to miss blue-sky moments because of habits that used to rob us of joy in the moment. When life gives us a magnificent time, we owe it to ourselves to revel in it, pushing away the worry that it won't last.

Part of our new spirituality involves believing we deserve the good things that come our way.

This is what the Lord God showed me—
a basket of summer fruit.

—Amos 8:1

Taking Back Our Lives

Messages from Nature

It was spring, and I was in a difficult phase of counseling. Memories, sometimes in the form of flashbacks, were returning. No day passed without tears, and sometimes the tears lasted hours.

"There's only one thing harder than living through childhood abuse," a survivor friend told me, "and that's going back and working through it."

In our town a beautiful walking path winds around a river. Several times that spring while walking the path I spotted a heron in the water. A couple of times one glided in and landed near me.

Many spiritual traditions hold that God converses with humans through nature.

I mentioned to other people who are familiar with the river that I was observing herons, but they had never seen herons anywhere nearby and thought perhaps I was mistaken. A man who spends hours beside the river every day identifying birds told me he hadn't seen herons there for years.

"I wish I'd see your heron," a friend said to me one day as we walked the river path together. Just then, a heron walked out of the bushes and posed near us. I felt pleased and vindicated.

I went searching for information about herons and learned that they are extremely patient. They stand very still watching for fish. When the moment is right, they pierce the water with their long beaks and make their catch.

Many spiritual traditions hold that God converses with humans through nature. When we're particularly in need of encouragement, we may find it useful to open our eyes and look for messages in God's creation, unexpected as they might be.

In that particularly troubled time, God's herons offered me an example of how patient waiting can be the perfect attitude for survivors of childhood abuse.

---

*The truly wise person kneels at the feet of all creatures
and is not afraid to endure the mockery of others.*
—Mechtilde of Magdeburg

Respecting Children

I was speaking to a group of schoolchildren, and a boy mentioned that *The Lion, the Witch and the Wardrobe* is his favorite book. I asked him why. "I like that four kids are the heroes and get to have all the adventures," the youngster responded.

"Why do you think the author made the heroes and heroines children?" I asked the class.

An owlish-looking ten-year-old threw up his hand. "Because it's about time we got some respect," he said.

I suppressed a smile, but another part of me felt sobered.

In the peaceful town where I live, the newspaper in recent months has reported stories about a mother convicted for beating to death her fifteen-month-old toddler, a suspected murder/arson that killed a child, and a man accused of murdering his girlfriend's infant.

"Isn't it about time children get respect?"

My friends who are schoolteachers experience times of despair dealing with the neglect and abuse of students. Those of us who were abused as children feel particularly sensitive about this issue.

We may ask, along with the owlish-looking boy, "Isn't it about time children get respect?" Our concern may lead us to join organizations that fight abuse, involve ourselves in youth programs, or support legislation aimed at protecting children. Or our stand may be a private one: we may combat the evil of child abuse by practicing respectful and loving treatment of our own children and of the children whose lives touch ours.

We can let our compassion for suffering children translate into action by taking personal stands to give children the respect they deserve.

"Let the little children come to me...
for it is to such as these
that the kingdom of heaven belongs."
—Matthew 19:14

Bonding by Belittling

Do you find yourself the brunt of jokes? Does your family tease you in ways that sting? Do coworkers team up to chide you? Is the role of buffoon one you step into with ease?

In some families the role of scapegoat falls on one child, and that child gets a big share of teasing or abuse. Children in other families alternate performing the role of sad clown. Other family members, relieved that they aren't the target, chime in to help humiliate the one being mocked. It's "bonding by belittling."

Healing involves casting new roles for ourselves if the old ones have been destructive to our self-worth.

It is unfortunate that some of us stay in the "family idiot" role for decades. So when we find ourselves the butt of sarcasm or putdowns, we need to take note. It is imperative to insist on respectful treatment. Jokes are funny only if they don't hurt anyone at any level.

Healing involves casting new roles for ourselves if the old ones have been destructive to our self-worth. Valuing ourselves is an important part of acknowledging how valuable we are in the Creator's sight.

Our resurrection does not lie wholly in the future;
it is also within us;
it is starting now;
it is already started.

—Paul Claudel

Making Peace
with Mystery

We want to figure it out, and we may grow compulsive about figuring it out. What did my abuse mean? Why did my abuse affect me differently than it did my siblings? Did abuse strengthen me in some way? Did God allow the abuse to happen for a greater good? Why does God allow evil at all?

The need to comprehend what happened to us may have followed us from childhood. Living with chaos, we may have put great energy into figuring out what was going on around us.

Looking at our pasts and asking questions may be part of our healing.

Many of us concluded that we were the ones who were bad. If we believed that, then the treatment we received made sense. Some of us concluded that our caretakers were wrong, which left us feeling the savage sting of injustice, but without recourse. Sometimes figuring it out got too hard, and we dealt with the issue of why by not dealing with it at all and numbing out.

Looking at our pasts and asking questions may be part of our healing. We may find, for example, that abuse has plagued our families for generations and that certain addictions have complicated the situation. Understanding details such as these may ease some of the hurt.

But what if answers elude us or seem insufficient? Eventually, we may have to make peace with mystery. If we find ourselves putting so much effort into solving the whys that we miss the gift of today, we may need to surrender some intellectual understanding and simply affirm in faith that our lives have meaning and purpose.

Today, while opening ourselves to healing, we can trust that our lives and histories are part of a greater plan. We don't need to understand every facet of it at this moment. We just need to recognize that it is so.

In an enchanted world,
one doesn't allow the magic to slip away
through any anxious demand for certainty.
—Thomas Moore

Staying Present

We had paired up at tai chi class for sparring, and my partner and I had hold of each other's forearms. Noting my fingers starting to tighten on his arm, he asked, "What's this tension?"

"I think you're getting ready to do something," I said.

"In this discipline, there is no place for anticipation. If you have fears from the past or anticipate the future, you telegraph it and give me an advantage. Stay relaxed and stay in the present."

Our past plays messages for us that cloud our present moments.

Sound advice—not just for tai chi practitioners but also for those healing from child abuse. How often we lose present moments because of fear of the past or anticipation of future hurts. We find ourselves spoiling the present in our relationships, on our jobs and even in routine situations. A friend of mine, for example, worries when she drives slowly on icy roads, fearing she is angering the driver behind her, whom she has never met and likely never will.

Our past plays messages for us that cloud our present

moments:

Love never works out. Love always means pain and betrayal. I will get hurt; I always do.

The boss knows I'm really not capable. Someone else could have done it better. Even now, she's trying to mask disapproval of me.

Things look pretty good in my life right now, but that won't last. I can't count on anything.

When we find ourselves returning to the past or moving ahead into the future, the best thing we can do for ourselves is realize that we've left the present. We don't have to berate ourselves or force change. Merely noticing that we have strayed returns us to the present, and the present has power and truth.

My times are in your hand.

—Psalm 31:15

Becoming Stargazers

he ancient Mayan civilization developed a calendar more accurate than our current one in reflecting the movement of the planets. Visitors to Mayan ruins learn how this happened.

Atop a Mayan pyramid lived a caste of priests who slept during the day and moved about only at night. Because their eyes were so adapted to darkness, they were able to perceive the tiniest bits of light in the heavens. Without modern telescopes, they learned a great deal about astronomy.

As children, many of us lived with a great deal of emotional darkness.

This is a great metaphor for the spirituality of survivors of abuse. As children, many of us lived with a great deal of emotional darkness, and in that darkness we learned to recognize pinpoints of lights in the heavens. As a result, we may have a deeper knowledge of God than those who grew up with bright light.

We do not want to be Pollyannaish about our childhoods. We want to admit to the sadness we carry because of our early years, but we also want to be grateful for the sweetness of knowing the map of heaven in a unique way.

When I look at your heavens, the work of your fingers,
the moon and the stars that you have established;
what are human beings that you are mindful of them,
mortals that you care for them?
Yet you have made them a little lower
than God, and crowned them with glory and honor.

—Psalm 8:3-5

≈≈

Joining the Battle for Truth

As we grew from being strong survivor children into worrying, fearful adults, we may have forgotten how tough and indestructible we are. However much it hurts to go back and look at our pain, the journey is nonetheless worthwhile. It lets us see how strong we were through those experiences and how strong we are today in our efforts to heal. Because we lived so long with self-blame and shame, believing that if someone abused us we must have deserved it, we have easily forgotten our innate goodness and strength.

God's Spirit is putting a shield in our hand that will swell our heart with bravery.

A force for good is working in our age to bring the evils of child abuse to light, and we survivors are taking part in that battle. We are ready, and God's Spirit is putting a shield in our hand that will swell our heart with bravery. Perhaps right now, the battle is for your own truth, but someday you may choose to join in the larger battle for truth-for-all.

Deep inside us, we've known we were warriors. We behaved as such as children. Whether we made it through by being inconspicuous, plucky, adaptive or defiant, we bravely made it through. We did not choose to die. Maybe we knew we had work ahead of us. Now we're undertaking it with God's help.

But you do see! Indeed, you note trouble and grief,
that you may take it into your hands:
the helpless commit themselves to you;
you have been the helper of the orphans.

—Psalm 10:14

≈≈

Attractive Scars

My daughter Mary and I were riding on an Amtrak train. A few rows behind us, a mother was arguing with a toddler. "You brat!" the woman screamed. "I'm gonna leave you beside the tracks when the train stops." That, of course, made the child shriek. The mother then whacked the child, and the sound of flesh hitting flesh caused tears to well in my eyes.

"I am," the woman continued to threaten. "I'm going to leave you by the tracks!"

"No, Momma, please, no!" the child pleaded.

The next stop was our destination. When Mary and I got off the train, I said, "Just in time. I couldn't have stood that much longer." Mary, twelve years old at the time, looked at me. "Stood what?" she asked.

"Didn't you hear that mother and child? The kid was crying her heart out."

Mary shrugged. "You must have sensitive hearing."

Youthful self-absorption may have been the reason Mary didn't hear the ruckus. The book she was reading may have held her enthralled. But the most engaging book in the world couldn't have shut out for me the sound of that child's anguish.

When we survivors of child abuse look back on our painful history, we wonder what life would have been like if we'd been raised within the embrace of safety and gentleness. Although we can be wistful for a different sort of childhood, it is almost certain that our early experiences developed in us traits we otherwise wouldn't have.

It is almost certain that our early experiences developed in us traits we otherwise wouldn't have.

Maybe we wouldn't have ears trained to hear the cries of hurting children. Maybe we wouldn't be as deeply empathetic to the pains of others. In a suffering world, our delicate sensitivities can be excellent traits.

Some of the scars we bear, it turns out, are attractive—albeit earned at a heavy price. Some of the things we endured marked us in ways that are positive for us and for others.

"Let anyone with ears to hear listen!"
—Luke 8:8

Honest Vulnerability

As survivors of child abuse, we have an ability to swallow disappointment, straighten our shoulders and push on. We know how to pick ourselves up, ignore our bruises and get on with things. We don't admit it, but we actually feel a bit superior about our ability to do this.

We can feel justly proud. As children, we learned skills that serve us well as adults. After all, isn't it good to be a person who copes well? Isn't it good to "take it on the chin" and not collapse under duress?

If we let down for even a minute, what might happen?

But some days we feel tired. Couldn't someone pick us up once in a while, or at least notice how courageously we've carried on? Couldn't we sink into a chair and let someone else take a turn at being strong? Because being strong and brave is a lonely business, resentment and burnout may be grabbing at us.

Our strong and brave act has its roots in denial, and it masks fear. If we let down for even a minute, what might happen?

We can keep the positive side of this behavior, but modify

the harmful side effects. We can appreciate our toughness while admitting to our vulnerability and humanness. We can admit to feeling tired, angry and scared, knowing that we are no less strong because of that admission.

We feel uneasy admitting to our frailties, but one of the bravest actions we can take on our own behalf is asking for help. "I need to unburden." "I feel so scared right now." "I need a good cry." "Could I have a hug?"

Practice this new and courageous honesty. Yes, it is human to feel vulnerable, and we exercise strength and bravery when we admit this.

---

*"Come to me all you that are weary
and are carrying heavy burdens,
and I will give you rest."*
—Matthew 11:28

Live in Abundant Light

Our turtle, Fluffy, became increasingly lethargic as winter days shortened. The UV light above his glass cage had burned out, and the neighborhood store didn't have any UV bulbs in stock. Fluffy stopped eating and didn't even come out of his cardboard box for a drink.

I scoured a number of stores and found a replacement light. But for a week, Fluffy stayed in his box, which I tilted upward so the light could reach him.

Then, well into the second week, Fluffy finally lumbered out of his box one morning, reared up on his hind legs and pushed against the glass. When I offered him a worm, he devoured it. After that, he was back to his active self.

We humans can suffer from lack of light, too.

A turtle needs UV light for the health of its shell, good digestion and overall maximum functioning. We humans can suffer from lack of light, too, both natural light and divine light.

For a time, those of us who are survivors of childhood abuse lived apart from the Light of God. Abuse may have discouraged us from seeking the light and may even have caused us to withdraw from it.

We now have Light again in our lives, manifesting itself as the desire to heal. The Light shows us we are deserving, lovable and cared for. With an abundance of Light, we become energetic creatures again.

Lead, kindly Light, amid the encircling gloom,
Lead thou me on;
The night is dark, and I am far from home,
Lead thou me on.
Keep Thou my feet; I do not ask to see
The distant scene; one step enough for me.

—John Henry Newman

Golden Opportunities

The woman looked to be forty or fifty, but she had the mental age of a young child. She wandered away from her family and came over to sit with me and a friend as we visited on a park bench. The woman's fingers suddenly dug into my arm, and she gave a shriek of alarm as a beautiful golden retriever came bounding toward us, ears flying, tail wagging.

"It's all right," I reassured the woman. "It's a very nice dog."

We cannot tell a beautiful, golden opportunity from the hurtful situations we once knew.

"I got bit by a dog once!" she said with a whimper.

The dog's owner caught up with the animal, apologized and put it on a leash. When the woman left to rejoin her family, my friend observed that it was unfortunate the woman couldn't enjoy an obviously friendly dog because of a bad episode with a mean one.

We survivors of child abuse can be like the woman. When we were young, we made judgments about the world based on our narrow experiences. Although we have grown up, the memory of early "bites" continues to infect us still. Sometimes when love charges toward us, hoping we'll be happy to see it, we actually cringe. We cannot tell a beautiful, golden opportunity from the hurtful situations we once knew.

It takes thoughtful awareness for us to stop and allow our adult selves to evaluate the present situation and decide whether we need to flinch. If we can calm our insides and see that we don't need to judge the present by the past, we may be able to turn toward the opportunity and embrace it.

It makes us, or it mars us.
—Shakespeare, *King Lear*

Hope, Anyway

You hit a day when you feel hopeless. You say to yourself, "I thought I'd made progress. But right now I can't believe that anything will ever change."

Then, quickly, you reprimand yourself. "I'm supposed to stay positive. The books/counselor/group all say that positive thinking is important."

When we are discouraged and are tempted to feel guilty about it, we must stop and remember an important fact about our background: hope often didn't pay off for us.

As frightened, abused children, we put hope in dreams that never materialized.

As a child, my friend believed that Julie Andrews, who became the mother of all those motherless "Sound of Music" children, would appear in her troubled life and make everything wonderful. When I was a child I had my own fantasy: I clung to a belief that one day I'd find a beautiful, sleek horse tied near my house, ride away on him, and everyone would miss me terribly.

As frightened, abused children, we put hope in dreams that

never materialized. One woman told of hiding during a game of hide-and-seek at a family picnic, hoping her family would be worried and search for her. Instead, hours passed, the picnic ended, and the family drove off without noticing she was missing. Another woman offered a chilling story of being left with a loaded gun when she was four years old, with instructions from her drunken parents to shoot any intruders. Although she prayed with all her might that her parents wouldn't get in the car and actually leave, they did just that.

When finding hope is a struggle for us, can we be kind to ourselves? Can we admit that hope scares us? If we can just be that honest with ourselves, we can go ahead and hope anyway.

Hope is the thing with feathers—
That perches in the soul—
And sings the tune without the words
And never stops—at all.

—Emily Dickinson

Unmasking Abuse

Some of us lived in families that looked picture-perfect. Combed and shiny family members filled a church pew on worship day, and those of us who lived with terror all week had to listen to neighbors tell us what a wonderful family we had. As a result, we dissociated from what was happening to us in the privacy of our home.

On the other hand, some of us lived in families that were clearly dysfunctional. We, too, often dissociated as a way to cope.

Today society is changing and saying that children must never be hurt.

In either case, looking at past abuse involves giving up untruths so we can grieve over the truth.

In our culture today, we are bringing to light the evil of child abuse. In an earlier time, the author Charles Dickens helped his culture look at the evil of child labor and other forms of child abuse. Abolitionists helped U.S. society look at the wickedness of slavery. Today society is changing and saying that children must never be hurt.

Can I believe that I, as an individual, have a role in this campaign for children? It doesn't need to be a public role; I can face my truth in solitude. I can quietly make a vow that the cycle of fear and abuse that has marked my family for generations will stop with me.

Today the Spirit of Truth is moving over our land. We can choose to cooperate with it to unmask the tragedy of child abuse. We can be brave partners to this Spirit by facing our own truths.

Those who would, may reach the upmost height—
but they must be eager to learn.

—The Buddha

Standing for Truth

When I attended the funeral of a Polish Solidarity worker who was exiled to the United States, I listened to the man's son read a tribute to his father's years in prison and later deportation. The man's stand for freedom had cost him dearly: the years in prison had damaged his health; he and his family had lost their homeland and the companionship of their close-knit families; and adjusting to the language, customs and culture of the land they came to was difficult and painful.

I wondered, however, if the man's family always felt supportive of him.

I told the son later, "I feel honored to have known your father. He was a hero of our era." The son responded in an emphatic way reminiscent of his father: "He was a hero. What we started swept across Eastern Europe, and Communism fell. It wasn't right that people couldn't have unions. It wasn't right that we couldn't go to church."

I smiled to hear the son say we, because he was only a boy when the trouble occurred. He was correct, of course, because the father's stand had an impact on the entire family, and the father's courage was his legacy.

I wondered, however, if the man's family always felt supportive of him. Weighing the costs, did they sometimes wish he would modify his positions? When his life was in danger, did his wife look at raising two children alone and wish she'd married someone less outspoken? In their early days as immigrants in this country, when they longed for familiar streets and a comprehensible tongue, did the family wonder if the actions of their loyal Solidarity-member husband and father had cost them too dearly?

> *Perhaps truth—and standing for truth—is the most worthwhile legacy we can leave our children.*

Occasionally, we stand in the company of someone who has risked everything to make the world more humane. We are in holy space at those times.

Survivors of child abuse sometimes struggle against family opposition, love of the status quo, and those who insist we "let bygones be bygones." Survivors of abuse can find themselves feeling mighty lonely.

At such times we must remind ourselves that standing for truth is a great and honorable undertaking. It may bring inconvenience and even pain to others, but ultimately, the truth is worth it. Perhaps truth—and standing for truth—is the most worthwhile legacy we can leave our children.

Our epitaphs probably won't read "Here Lies Fred, Who Stood for Truth" or "Here Is Jane. The Cycle of Abuse Stopped with Her." Such personal heroics may not be noted, but their impact is monumental.

---

*"Remove the sandals from your feet,
for the place on which you are standing
is holy ground."*

—Exodus 3:5

Interrupting the Cycle

 memorial stone, planted beside a popular walking path in our small community, reads: "To honor all survivors of child abuse and those who have chosen to break the cycle and become celebrators of life."

A survivor friend and I have often stood beside this stone in silence, arms linked in reverent solidarity. Sometimes the stone, which looks something like a grave marker, has flowers placed beside it. I like the fact that the rock looks like a tombstone; I want to see child abuse die.

Sometimes my own healing has hurt so much that I've wondered if the effort today could be worth the results tomorrow. I wanted to return to the familiar numbness of denial that I knew for so many years. Then I would remember the words on the memorial marker about breaking the cycle.

When we heal, we help stop the cycle.

Programs to educate and alert the public about abuse are helping to break the cycle. Those of us working to heal from its effects are helping too. Abuse may have haunted our families for generations, and maybe we have even perpetuated it ourselves. When we heal, though, we help stop the cycle.

Healing is a courageous path to walk. At those times when we want to turn away from that arduous path, we can remember that our work isn't just for ourselves. Rather, it's for the world as well. When we bloom into confident, fulfilled persons, individuals who stand in and for the truth, we give the world a valuable gift.

Did our Creator intend us to shrink from life? No. God celebrates when we come out of our cocoons, stretch our limbs and try our wings. When we begin to soar, we do it not just for ourselves, not just for our loved ones. We soar for the world.

Today I have set before you
life and death, blessings and curses.
Choose life, so that you and your descendants may live.
—Deuteronomy 30:19

Also from ACTA Publications

Protect Us from All Anxiety
Meditations for the Depressed
by William Burke
drawings by Mary Southard
The bestselling book of fifty powerful spiritual reflections on severe
and chronic depression by a priest who suffers from bi-polar disorder himself. (128-page paperback, ISBN: 0-87946-184-5, $9.95)

Freedom from Fear
Overcoming Anxiety through Faith
By Marci Alborghetti
Forty faith-based reflections for those who suffer from general anx-
iety, unresolved fear or panic attacks. (160-page paperback, ISBN:
0-87946-231-0, $9.95)

The Light Within
A Woman's Book of Solace
By Joni Woelfel
Each of these forty reflections is combined with a scripture passage
and an original heartfelt prayer for women experiencing hardship
of any kind. (128-page paperback, ISBN: 0-87946-208-6, $9.95)

Tear Soup
A Recipe for Healing after Loss
By Pat Schwiebert and Chuck DeKlyen
Illustrated by Taylor Bills
A modern-day fable—told in a richly illustrated children's book for-
mat suitable for children and adults—about a woman who has suf-
fered a terrible but unnamed loss. (60-page hardcover, ISBN: 0-
9615197-6-2, $19.95)

Available from booksellers
or 800-397-2292 or www.actapublications.com